TRIBUTE TO TAYLOR HAWKINS

REMEMBERING TAYLOR HAWKINS

STELLA O. MAURICE

Copyright ©2022 Stella O. Maurice
All Rights Reserved

Table of Contents

CHAPTER 1 6
BIOGRAPHY OF TAYLOR HAWKINS 6
    CHAPTER 2 10
PROFESSION 10
HAWKINS SIDE SCHEME 14
    CHAPTER 3 20
MOTIVATORS 20
MARRIAGE 20
    CHAPTER 4 24
HAWKIN'S DEMISE 24
    CHAPTER 5 28
CARDIOVASCULAR COLLAPSE 28
INDICATORS OF CARDIOVASCULAR COLLAPSE ... 30
    CHAPTER 6 32
WHEN TO SEE A HEALTH SPECALIST 32
    CHAPTER 7 36
CAUSES OF CARDIOVASCULAR COLLAPSE 36
    CHAPTER 8 40
HEART CONDITIONS THAT CAN PROMPT SUDDEN CARDIAC ARREST 40

RISK CHARACTERISTICS 43
    CHAPTER 9 46
INTRICACIES OF CARDIOVASCULAR COLLAPSE 46
DETERRENCE OF CARDIOVASCULAR COLLAPSE 46
    CHAPTER 10 48
TRIBUTE TO TAYLOR HAWKINS 48

CHAPTER 1

BIOGRAPHY OF TAYLOR HAWKINS

Oliver Taylor Hawkins was an American artist who was brought into the world in Fort Worth, Texas, on February 17, 1972. His family moved to Laguna Beach, California, in 1976, where Hawkins grew up. Hawkins was the minor of three, with older siblings, Jason, and Heather. He moved on from Laguna Beach High School in 1990, where he had been companions with the ebb and flow Yes lead entertainer Jon Davison.

Hawkins was most popular as the drummer of the musical crew Foo Fighters, with whom he recorded nine studio albums somewhere in the range of 1999 and 2021. Before joining the band in 1997, he was the touring drummer for Sass Jordan and Alanis Morissette, as well as the drummer in the ever-evolving exploratory band Sylvia.

Hawkins joined the Foo Fighters in 1997 after beforehand filling in as the drummer for Alanis Morissette's band and touring with them on the side of their collection "The Color and the Shape," which was additionally delivered that year.

In 2004, Hawkins established his side task, 'Taylor Hawkins and the Coattail Riders', in which he played drums and sang, delivering three studio albums between the range of 2006 and 2019. He established the supergroup NHC with Jane's Addiction members Dave

Navarro and Chris Chaney in 2020, where he additionally took on lead vocal and drumming obligations.

Hawkins was enlisted into the Rock and Roll Hall of Fame in 2021 as an individual from Foo Fighters. He was appointed "Best Rock Drummer" in 2005 by the British drumming magazine Rhythm.

CHAPTER 2

PROFESSION

Hawkins played in the Orange County-based band Sylvia before he turned into the drummer for Sass Jordan.

From June 1995 until March 1997, Hawkins was Alanis Morissette's drummer on the tour supporting 'Jagged Little Pill' and 'Can't Not Tour'. He appeared in the recordings for "You Oughta Know", "All I Really Want", and "You Learn". He additionally showed up on Morissette's VHS/DVD Jagged Little Pill, Live (1997).

In the wake of touring through the spring of 1996, Foo Fighters entered a Seattle studio with producer Gil Norton to record their subsequent album. Dispute supposedly emitted during recording between Dave Grohl and drummer William Goldsmith, ultimately provoking Goldsmith to leave the band. The band pulled together in Los Angeles and re-recorded the collection with Grohl on drums. The album, The Color, and the Shape were delivered on May 20, 1997. Grohl called Hawkins, a colleague at that point, wanting his suggestions for another drummer to join the band. Grohl was convinced, possibly by mistake, that Hawkins wouldn't leave Morissette's touring band, given he was a greater demonstration than Foo Fighters at that point. Shockingly, notwithstanding, Hawkins proposed to join the band himself, clarifying that he needed to be a drummer in a rock band as opposed to a solo act. The band declared Hawkins would be its new drummer on March 18, 1997. Hawkins initially showed up with the

Foo Fighters in the music video for the 1997 single "Monkey Wrench", albeit the song was recorded before he joined the band.

Notwithstanding his drumming with the Foo Fighters, Hawkins additionally gave vocals, guitar, and piano to different recordings. He played out the lead vocal on the cover of Pink Floyd's "Have a Cigar". Two editions of the song were delivered, one as the B-side to "Learn to Fly" and one more on the Mission: Impossible 2 soundtrack album. He later sang lead vocals on "Cold Day in the Sun" from In Your Honor, which was subsequently delivered as a single, as well as a cover of Cream's "I Feel Free", which showed up as the B-side of "DOA" and on the EP Five Songs and a Cover. Hawkins additionally sang lead vocals for the band's cover of Joe

Walsh's "Life of Illusion". Afterward, he sang lead vocals for "Sunday Rain", a track on the Foo Fighters' 2017 album Concrete and Gold. He sang lead vocals on certain songs during Foo Fighters' live shows, like a Cover of Queen's "Someone To Love" at his last show with the band. He likewise added to the band's songwriting and was recorded as a co-writer on each album since 'There Is Nothing Left to Lose'.

Hawkins' last performance with the Foo Fighters before his demise was at the Lollapalooza Argentina festival on March 20, 2022. Hawkins after his death won three Grammys with the Foo Fighters on April 3, 2022

HAWKINS SIDE SCHEME

In 2006, Hawkins delivered a self-titled LP with his side project, Taylor Hawkins and the Coattail Riders. Taylor Hawkins and the Coattail Riders later delivered two more studio albums: Red Light Fever in 2010, and Get the Money in 2019. He sometimes played with a Police cover band on the other hand called "The Cops" and "Fallout". At Live Earth in 2007, Hawkins was important for SOS Allstars with Roger Taylor of Queen and Chad Smith of Red Hot Chili Peppers.

Hawkins recorded the drum tracks for the Coheed and Cambria collection Good Apollo, I'm Burning Star IV, Volume Two: No World for Tomorrow as the band's standard drummer, Chris Pennie, couldn't record on account of legally binding reasons. Hawkins likewise toured with Coheed and Cambria momentarily during the months of the album. Hawkins can likewise be heard drumming on Eric Avery's (previously of Jane's Addiction) first independent solo, Help Wanted, and on Kerry Ellis' album, Wicked in Rock. Hawkins and Grohl divide drumming obligations on Harmony & Dissidence, the third collection by Foo Fighter's bandmate Chris Shiflett's side project, Jackson United.

Hawkins played on the track "Cyborg", from Queen guitarist Brian May's 1998 solo collection, Another World; he likewise played drums at VH1's Rock Honors 2006 while Queen performed "We Will Rock You". He sang backing vocals on the Queen + Paul Rodgers single, "C-celebrity".

Hawkins was assigned to finish an incomplete recording of a song by Beach Boys' drummer Dennis Wilson named "Holy Man" by composing and singing new verses. The recording, which likewise highlighted contribution from Brian May and Roger Taylor of Queen, was given as a single for Record Store Day in 2019.

While the Foo Fighters were on break in 2013, Hawkins established a Rock cover band called Chevy Metal. Hawkins showed up on Slash's solo album Slash, delivered in 2010, giving backing vocals on the track "Crucify the Dead", featuring Ozzy Osbourne.

In 2013, he made his acting debut in the position of Iggy Pop in the rock film CBGB. Hawkins recorded the drums on Vasco Rossi's last song, "L'uomo più semplice". This melody was delivered on January 21, 2013, in Italy.

In March 2014, Hawkins openly declared his new side scheme called 'The Birds of Satan'. It includes Hawkins' drum specialist and bandmate from Chevy Metal, Wiley Hodgden on bass and vocals as well as guitarist Mick Murphy also of Chevy Metal. The band's self-titled debut collection was delivered in April 2014, with a delivery party at 'Rock n Roll Pizza' highlighting the Foo Fighters guesting on a portion of the cover tracks.

In a meeting with Radio X, Hawkins disclosed that his primary thought for his performance projects was to duet with female artists.

Hawkins welcomed different stars to sing in the Taylor Hawkins and the Coattail Riders album 'Get the Money', for example, LeAnn Rimes, who sang on one of his songs named "C U In Hell". Loud wire titled the collection one of the 50 best Rock efforts of 2019. Different performers who showed up at his activities included Roger Taylor, Brian May, Dave Grohl, Nancy Wilson, Joe Walsh, Chrissie Hynde, and some more.

In October 2021 Elton John delivered The Lockdown Sessions, which highlighted Hawkins playing drums on the song "E-Ticket".

In 2021, Hawkins and Jane's Addiction members Dave Navarro and Chris Chaney established a supergroup called NHC. Portrayed by Hawkins as being "somewhere between Rush and the Faces", the band made its live debut in September 2021 at Eddie Vedder's Ohana celebration, with Taylor's Foo Fighters bandmate Pat

Smear on extra guitar. The band recorded a collection in 2021, which is expected for release in 2022.

Alongside different individuals from Foo Fighters, Hawkins featured as himself in the comedy horror film Studio 666, delivered on February 25, 2022.

CHAPTER 3

MOTIVATORS

Hawkins' initial two significant motivations were Roger Taylor and Stewart Copeland. He revealed that paying attention to these two drummers' various styles showed him a wide range of drumming styles. He additionally referenced that he would play along with songs on the radio or records, for example: Queen's News of the World, to upgrade his abilities when he was young.

MARRIAGE

Hawkins and his wife, Alison, wedded in 2005 and they have three children. They lived in Hidden Hills, California, in the wake of moving from Topanga Canyon in 2012.

Hawkins abused heroin in August 2001, which left him in a state of unconsciousness for 2 weeks. Hawkins' bandmate and closest companion, Dave Grohl, stayed with him in the hospital in London for a very long time until he awakened. Grohl said he was prepared to stop the music while Hawkins was in the medical clinic. He likewise disclosed in the 2011 documentary Foo Fighters: Back and Forth, that he composed the song "On The Mend" from the band's 2005's collection In Your Honor, about Hawkins while he was in a state of unconsciousness. Addressing Beats 1 host Matt Wilkinson in 2018 about the episode, Hawkins said: "I was partying a lot. I wasn't an addict, essentially, yet I was celebrating. There was a year when the celebrating just got excessively enormous. One evening and I awakened going, 'What on earth occurred?' That was a truly changing point for me." In a same interview, Hawkins likewise said he was sober.

Hawkins experienced anxiety in front of large audiences. Talking about his wellbeing in a June 2021 interview with Rolling Stone magazine, Hawkins said; "I'm sound. I'm great... I get sinus infections downright horrendous. Furthermore, I just determined from my PCP, got all my blood tests and my heart everything checked and he goes, 'Fella, you're looking good. Your heart's large since you practice a great deal. It resembles a sprinter's heart.' And that is fine. Mainly, he said, 'I think you have sleep apnea.'

In his 2021 journal The Story Teller, Dave Grohl portrayed Hawkins as "my brother from another mother, my dearest companion, a person for whom I would take a bullet.

CHAPTER 4

HAWKIN'S DEMISE

On March 25, 2022, emergency services were called to the Four Seasons Casa Medina Hotel in Bogotá, Colombia, where Hawkins was experiencing chest pain in his lodging. Health personnel showed up and found Hawkins lethargic; they did CPR, however, he was pronounced dead at the scene, at 50 years old. No reason for death was given.

The next day, Colombian administrations declared that a preliminary urine toxicology test implied that Hawkins had ten substances in his system at the hour of his passing, including opioids, benzodiazepines, tricyclic antidepressants, and THC, a psychoactive compound in cannabis.

On the evening of his demise, Hawkins was slated to perform with the Foo Fighters at the Estéreo Picnic Festival in Bogotá as a component of their continuous South American tour. The Festival stage was transformed into a candlelight vigil for Hawkins.

It was said by the Columbia Principal legal officer that Taylor Hawkins had ten various narcotics in his system when he passed on. Marijuana, opiates, tricyclic antidepressants, and benzodiazepines were among the synthetic substances found by examiners during a urine toxicological test.

The typical load of a human heart in grown-up men is around 300 to 350 grams, Scientific specialists said

Hawkins' heart weighed very nearly 600 grams. This was found during the dissection. A heavier-than-ordinary heart weight might be related to cardiovascular illnesses including cardiomyopathy which makes it harder for the organ to siphon blood to the remainder of the body and can prompt cardiovascular breakdown.

Specialists have inferred that the 50-year-old experienced a cardiovascular breakdown after gorging on a mixed drink of pills.

CHAPTER 5

CARDIOVASCULAR COLLAPSE

The cardiovascular breakdown is extreme hypotension from critical disorder of the heart or fringe vasculature causing hypotension with stemming cerebral hypoperfusion and loss of cognizance that can be the outcome of a cardiovascular arrhythmia, serious myocardial or valvular disorder, loss of vascular tone, as well as intense disturbance of venous return. At the point when the viable course is reestablished unexpectedly, patients present with syncope. On the off chance that natural solution doesn't happen, then, at that point, heart failure happens, eventually bringing about death if revival endeavors are fruitless or not started.

Sudden Cardiac Arrest (SCA) alludes to a sudden loss of heart capability bringing about complete cardiovascular breakdown due either to an intense dangerous heart arrhythmia or unexpected loss of myocardial siphon capability that requires emergency medical interference for reclamation of compelling flow. Most SCAs happens outside the hospital, and less than 10% of these casualties overcome the crisis.

Sudden Cardiac Arrest isn't equivalent to a heart attack when the bloodstream to a piece of the heart is hindered. In any case, a heart attack can occasionally set off an electrical unsettling influence that prompts unexpected heart failure.

On the off chance that not treated right away, Sudden Cardiac Arrest can prompt death. Survival is apparent with quick, proper medical attention. Cardiopulmonary resuscitation (CPR), utilizing a defibrillator — or even giving compressions to the chest — can work on the possibilities of survival until emergency workers show up.

INDICATORS OF CARDIOVASCULAR COLLAPSE

Signs of Sudden Cardiac Arrest are prompt and exceptional and include:

- Abrupt breakdown
- No heartbeat
- No breathing
- Loss of cognizance

Once in a while, different signs and side effects happen before Sudden Cardiac Arrest. These could include:

- Chest pain
- Windedness- shortness of breath
- Frailty- weakness
- Quick pulsating, vacillating, or beating heart (palpitations)

However, sudden cardiac arrest frequently happens with no advance notice.

CHAPTER 6

WHEN TO SEE A HEALTH SPECALIST

Call 911 or emergency medical help assuming you experience any of these signs and indications:

- Chest pain or inconvenience
- Heart throbbing
- Quick or unpredictable pulses
- Unexplained wheezing
- Windedness- shortness of breath
- Swooning or close blacking out
- Discombobulation or unsteadiness

At the point when the heart stops, the absence of oxygen-rich blood can cause death or continual brain mind injury in practically no time. Time is crucial while you're helping an oblivious individual who isn't breathing.

If you see somebody who's oblivious and breathing abnormally, do the following:

- Call 911 or emergency medical help. On the off chance that you have prompt access to a phone, call before starting CPR.
- Do CPR. Immediately check the individual's breathing. On the off chance that the individual is breathing abnormally, start CPR. Push rigid and quick on the individual's chest — at the pace of 100 to 120 compressions every minute. Assuming you've been drilled in CPR, inspect the individual's airway and convey salvage/ rescue breaths after every 30 compressions.
- If you haven't been tutored, simply proceed with chest compressions. Permit the chest to rise totally

between compressions. Continue to do this until a versatile defibrillator is accessible or emergency staff show up.

- Utilize a compact defibrillator, on the off chance that one is accessible. It will give you bit-by-bit voice directions. Proceed with chest compressions while the defibrillator is charging. At the point when it's charged, the defibrillator will look at the individual's heart mood and suggest a shock if necessary. Convey one shock in the event prompted by the gadget and, quickly continue CPR, beginning with chest compressions, or giving chest compressions just, for around two minutes.
- Utilizing the defibrillator, inspect the individual's heartbeat. If crucial, the defibrillator will give

another shock. Reiterate this cycle until the individual recuperates cognizance or emergency workers dominate.

- Portable automated external defibrillators (AEDs) are accessible in many spots, including airports, gambling clubs, and shopping centers. You can likewise buy one for your home. AEDs arrive with built-in directions for their utilization. They're modified to permit a shock just when suitable.

CHAPTER 7

CAUSES OF CARDIOVASCULAR COLLAPSE

Call 911 or emergency medical help assuming you experience any of these signs and indications:

- Chest pain or inconvenience
- Heart throbbing
- Quick or unpredictable pulses
- Unexplained wheezing
- Windedness- shortness of breath
- Swooning or close blacking out
- Discombobulation or unsteadiness

At the point when the heart stops, the absence of oxygen-rich blood can cause death or continual brain mind injury in practically no time. Time is crucial while you're helping an oblivious individual who isn't breathing.

If you see somebody who's oblivious and breathing abnormally, do the following:

- Call 911 or emergency medical help. On the off chance that you have prompt access to a phone, call before starting CPR.
- Do CPR. Immediately check the individual's breathing. On the off chance that the individual is breathing abnormally, start CPR. Push rigid and quick on the individual's chest — at the pace of 100 to 120 compressions every minute. Assuming you've been drilled in CPR, inspect the individual's airway and convey salvage/ rescue breaths after every 30 compressions.
- If you haven't been tutored, simply proceed with chest compressions. Permit the chest to rise totally

between compressions. Continue to do this until a versatile defibrillator is accessible or emergency staff show up.

- Utilize a compact defibrillator, on the off chance that one is accessible. It will give you bit-by-bit voice directions. Proceed with chest compressions while the defibrillator is charging. At the point when it's charged, the defibrillator will look at the individual's heart mood and suggest a shock if necessary. Convey one shock in the event prompted by the gadget and, quickly continue CPR, beginning with chest compressions, or giving chest compressions just, for around two minutes.

- Utilizing the defibrillator, inspect the individual's heartbeat. If crucial, the defibrillator will give another shock. Reiterate this cycle until the individual recuperates cognizance or emergency workers dominate.

- Portable automated external defibrillators (AEDs) are accessible in many spots, including airports, gambling clubs, and shopping centers. You can likewise buy one for your home. AEDs arrive with built-in directions for their utilization. They're modified to permit a shock just when suitable.

CHAPTER 8

HEART CONDITIONS THAT CAN PROMPT SUDDEN CARDIAC ARREST

Abrupt heart failure can occur in individuals who have no known heart illness. Be that as it may, a perilous arrhythmia usually develops in an individual with a prior, perhaps undiscovered heart condition. These circumstances include:

- Coronary artery disease. Most instances of abrupt heart failure happen in individuals who have coronary artery disease, in which the arteries become obstructed with cholesterol and different stores, lessening the bloodstream to the heart.
- Cardiovascular failure. If a heart attack happens, frequently because of extreme coronary artery

disease, it can set off ventricular fibrillation and unexpected heart failure. Likewise, a heart failure can leave scar tissue in your heart. Electrical short circuits around the scar tissue can prompt anomalies in your heartbeat.

- Enlarged heart (cardiomyopathy). This happens principally when your heart's muscular walls stretch and develop or thicken. Then, at that point, your heart's muscle is unusual, a condition that frequently prompts arrhythmias.
- Valvular disease: Spilling or restricting of your heart valves can prompt extending or thickening of your heart muscle. At the point when the chambers become expanded or debilitated in light of pressure brought about by a tight or spilling valve, there's an increased chance of nurturing arrhythmia.

- Heart defect presents at birth (congenital heart disease). At the point when sudden cardiac arrest happens in youngsters or teenagers, it very well may be because of congenital heart disease. Grown-ups who've had corrective surgery for an intrinsic heart defect have a higher chance of sudden heart failure.
- Electrical issues in the heart. In certain individuals, the issue is in the heart's electrical framework itself rather than an issue with the heart muscle or valves. These are called primary heart rhythm anomalies and incorporate circumstances like Brugada syndrome and long QT syndrome.

RISK CHARACTERISTICS

Some risk characteristics of Cardiovascular Collapse are:

- Chambers and valves of the heart
- Chambers and valves of the heart open pop-up dialogue box

Since an unexpected cardiac arrest is so frequently connected with coronary conduit infection, the very factors that put you in danger of coronary artery diseases can likewise jeopardize your abrupt cardiac arrest. These include:

- Family chronology of coronary artery disease
- Smoking
- Hypertension
- High blood cholesterol

- Weight/ Plumpness
- Diabetes
- A sedentary way of life

Additional elements that could build your chance of sudden heart failure include:

- A prior episode of heart failure or family chronology of heart failure.
- An earlier cardiovascular collapse.
- An individual or family background of different types of heart disease, for example, heart rhythm disorder, congenital heart defects, heart failure and cardiomyopathy.
- Becoming an adult — the chance of unexpected heart failure rises with age.

- Being male.
- Utilizing illicit medications, like cocaine or amphetamines.
- Nutritional irregularity, for example, low potassium or magnesium levels
- Obstructive sleep/rest apnea
- Persistent kidney disease

CHAPTER 9

INTRICACIES OF CARDIOVASCULAR COLLAPSE

At the point when sudden cardiac arrest happens, decreased bloodstream to your mind causes swoon. If your heart rhythm doesn't quickly regulate, brain harm happens, and demise happens. Overcomers of heart failure could give indications of brain defect.

DETERRENCE OF CARDIOVASCULAR COLLAPSE

Curtail your chance of abrupt heart failure by doing conventional checkups, being examined for coronary disease, and carrying on with a heart-healthy way of life.

CHAPTER 10

TRIBUTE TO TAYLOR HAWKINS

Foo Fighters, Dave Chappelle, Stevie Nicks, Elton John, Jason Sudeikis, and more came together to respect the life and music of Taylor Hawkins last weekend.

The deceased Foo Fighter drummer, who passed on abruptly while on a tour to Colombia in March, was commemorated by his dear companions, family, and fans at the first of two recognition shows in London's Wembley Arena on Saturday. A subsequent concert will be held stateside at the Kia Forum in Los Angeles on Sept. 27.

Affectionately intertwined, the Foo Fighters opened the occasion with a strong discourse conveyed by front man Dave Grohl.

The band was then joined on stage by Liam Gallagher, who played the Oasis spring hits "Rock 'N' Roll Star" and "Live Forever."

In a voice message played during the occasion, rock legend Stevie Nicks read the compliment she wrote for Hawkins back in March when she joined the Foo Fighters for a practice. "We recorded a kickass rendition of 'Gold Dust Woman" life, and toward the end of the song, I shouted out, 'best "Gold Dust Woman" ever!' And I meant it."

Sudeikis showed up all through the night, including acquainting Supergrass with the stage, whom he remembered opened for the Foo Fighters when the Ted Lasso star saw the band in 1997. "It was likewise the first I got to see Taylor Hawkins perform live," he said.

During the occasion's elegant setup — which included performances by Wolfgang Van Halen, Rush, and the Pretenders — Dave Chappelle made that big appearance to recall Hawkins as both a melodic legend and a family man. The comedian met the Foo Fighters while facilitating Saturday Night Live back in November 2020, when he let the band know that his go-to karaoke song is Radiohead's 1992 hit "Creep.

At the tribute occasion, Shane, 16, joined his late dad's bandmates performed "My Legend." It was an emotional scene.

The Foo Fighters finished off the night by playing a variety of their hits — including "Learn to Fly," "Best of You," and "Times like These" — with an alternating cast of drummers, including Blink-182 rocker Travis Barker, Rufus Taylor, and 12-year-old Nandi Bushell.

The show highlighted performances from a portion of Hawkins' favorite bands and musicians, including Metallica, Rush, Supergrass, and Stewart Copeland of The Police.

"The most recent couple of days, we have been asking ourselves a similar question after each practice: 'I can't help thinking about what Taylor would consider of this - to see these incredible individuals together making music?'" expressed Grohl at a certain point, again attempting to contain his feelings.

Printed in Great Britain
by Amazon